PANNELL LIBRARY

S0-BFD-192

Boise State University Western Writers Series   Number 71

Charles Sealsfield

By Walter Grünzweig

Karl-Franzens-Universität Graz, Austria

PT
2516
.S4
Z863
1985

Editors: Wayne Chatterton
James H. Maguire

Business Manager:
James Hadden

Cover Design and Illustration
by Arny Skov, Copyright 1985

Boise State University, Boise, Idaho

71748

Copyright 1985
by the
Boise State University Western Writers Series

ALL RIGHTS RESERVED

Library of Congress Card No. 85-70131

International Standard Book No. 0-88430-045-5

Printed in the United States of America by
Boise State University Printing and Graphics Services
Boise, Idaho

Charles Sealsfield

Charles Sealsfield

I.

The death of an aging, terminally ill American in the small city of Solothurn, Switzerland, on 26 May 1864, did not receive much public attention at first. Charles Sealsfield had lived on his small estate for some six years and was generally regarded as an eccentric, a writer who had known fame in his earlier days but who had long since resigned himself to a peaceful existence in Switzerland, one of the few non-autocratic countries in Europe at that time. To everyone's surprise, however, the execution of his last will revealed that the old writer was not born in Pennsylvania, as his U.S. passport indicated, but in Poppitz, a small village in Southern Moravia, then part of the Austro-Hungarian Empire (today Czechoslovakia). It appeared that his true name was Karl Postl, that he was born in Poppitz in the year 1793, and that his father, Anton Postl, was a farmer in the same village, employed by a monastic order with headquarters in Prague.

Reporters and literary journalists, especially in the German-language areas of Europe where Sealsfield's works had been highly successful, soon became interested in the extraordinary life of Sealsfield-Postl, who seemed to be an Austrian farmer's son and a celebrated American writer at the same time. They also welcomed as sensational news the fact that Karl Postl had studied to be a priest, taken his vows as a monk and, for a time, held an important position as secretary of the monastic order of the Kreuzherren in Prague, the same order which had employed his father. Research into the files of the order, as well as the criminal records of the Austrian police, also showed that in 1823 Sealsfield had broken his vow and escaped to the United States. Although there were "Wanted" notices throughout the Empire following his disappearance, neither Metternich's secret police nor other governmental authorities managed to intercept him.

Given the great number of fascinating details making up Sealsfield's biography until the age of thirty, it comes as no surprise that subsequent scholars were interested in probing more and more deeply into the writer's later life as well. Towards the close of the nineteenth century, the tendency to make a writer's biography the primary focus in literary criticism reenforced this direction in Sealsfield scholarship. This biographical orientation rendered impossible the adequate interpretation or even judgment of the work itself.

Insufficient attention to some twelve novels and numerous pieces of short prose also resulted in the failure to define Sealsfield's place in literature—both historically and geographically. His use of German in his fiction and the discovery of his place of birth and schooling—Sealsfield had gone to *Gymnasium* in Znaim and was subsequently a student at Prague—led to the unshakable belief that Sealsfield had to be a purely Austrian or German writer—in any case European.

In their eurocentrism, these scholars, some of them American, overlooked the possibility that Sealsfield's mind might have turned "American" in the course of his years spent in the New World. It was not until the late 1960s that the German critic and Sealsfield researcher, Alexander Ritter, suggested that with regard to structure and theme, Sealsfield's works bear a remarkable likeness to much of the American literature of his period. To be sure, some historians of American literature had known about Sealsfield for a long time, but they had, for the most part, only considered the novels published in English in the 1840s and were unaware of the author's multicultural background.

Ritter demanded that specialists in German *and* American literature cooperate on a critical and comparative evaluation of Sealsfield's works. Much of the research since then has shown the necessity of this approach. Sealsfield's works must indeed be judged from the European *and* American perspective as he is an Austrian-American writer whose work belongs, at least in part, to the tradition of ethnic American literature such as Polish-American or Italian-American writing.

The investigation of Sealsfield's fiction in the context of American thought and literature shows that the Austrian immigrant did not confine himself to the traditional literary genres inspired by eighteenth-century English neoclassicism then prevalent in much of the New World. Rather, he attempted to reach out across the Alleghenies, to include in his writing what Alexander Cowie has called the American writer's "unique assets": "territorial extent which dwarfed the British Isles . . . different climate, topography, and wild life . . . . He had the Indian—a new race to lend strength to a new literature. And he had a nation lately sprung into independence" (116). Rather than restricting himself to the traditions of the sentimental, gothic, or picaresque novels or even that of the tale of seduction, Sealsfield created his own version of Sir Walter Scott's historical romance which replaced the English writer's strictly historical subject matter by topics less removed in time. Sealsfield's great theme is the civilization of the country from East to West and in describing this process in fictional terms, he becomes one of the country's earliest Western writers—along with Timothy Flint,

7

James Hall, William Gilmore Simms, and other authors whose works he knew and used imaginatively in his own prose.

Sealsfield's metamorphosis from an Austrian monk to a Western American writer can only be explained in terms of his personal experience. At the time, Austria was a dismal place. Since 1819, political repression and surveillance had increased and Metternich, the extremely reactionary chancellor of the Empire, had installed an omnipresent and efficient secret police, which attempted to stamp out any form of internal, especially intellectual, dissent. Sealsfield, who seems to have been close to liberal circles in Prague continuing the Enlightenment tradition, must have felt particularly bitter about this development. In 1819, his liberal teacher Bernard Bolzano, a philosopher of religion, was brought to trial and removed from his position in the school of theology.

It therefore comes as no surprise that Sealsfield, following his arrival in the United States in 1823, allied himself with the more radically democratic and anti-European faction in American politics—the Jacksonian Democrats. Having arrived in New Orleans only nine years after Jackson's victory over the English in the "battle" of New Orleans, he could hear everywhere in the streets of the city the popular song "The Hunters of Kentucky," which praised Jackson and his western riflemen. Sealsfield's non-fictional work *The United States of North America as they are*, published in London in 1827 and designed to enlighten the British reader on the subject of the United States and her public life, shows that Sealsfield was very interested in the presidential elections of 1824. In the course of this campaign, Sealsfield must have come to know the politics of "Old Hickory" Jackson, "the head of the Radicals, who expected from his powerful hand a thorough reform of the administration" (*The United States of North America*, Complete Works 2, 9). Jackson was committed to fight the party of the "fashionables" and (in his view) Anglophiles headed by John Quincy Adams.

In 1824, Jackson lost against Adams; but already in 1826, marking the first half century of the existence of the United States, Jackson, who was thought by many to carry the torch of the American Revolution, was again in the forefront of public attention. *The United States*, published prior to the elections of 1828, clearly favors Jackson's renewed bid for the presidency. For Sealsfield, as for many other Americans, Jackson's presidency in 1829 marked a new era in American history. For the first time, the West had asserted itself as a politically relevant section, suggesting that in the future, America would be less inclined to look only towards the East and Europe.

Curiously enough, Jackson, a lawyer and planter-aristocrat from Tennessee, did not seem the born leader of the Western section of the country. He was not at all a "Hunter of Kentucky" or even a latter-day version of Daniel Boone. What makes Jackson's campaign and the years of his administration so interesting is the creation of a myth around his person. John William Ward describes Jackson as a "symbol of his age" and indeed, Jacksonian propaganda and ideology, as we can study it in contemporary documents, clearly has distinct literary, almost fictional qualities, which must have been appealing to a young, imaginative mind like Sealsfield's.

As strong as this influence may have been on the young European immigrant, it was not the only reason for Sealsfield's interest in the West. In a travel book titled *The Americans as they are; Described in a Tour through the Valley of the Mississippi*, also published in London in 1828, Sealsfield gives an account of an actual journey through Pennsylvania, Ohio, Kentucky, Indiana, Illinois, Missouri, Mississippi, Tennessee, Louisiana, and the territory of Arkansas.

He seems to have spent his summers in the North, in New York and especially Pennsylvania, a state with a large number of German settlers, and his winters in Louisiana. Following a short trip to Europe in 1827, he might have traveled to Mexico and, for a time, have owned a plantation on the Red River in Louisiana.

The seven years from 1823 until 1830 seem to have been formative for Sealsfield. His first novel, *Tokeah; or the White Rose*, was written in 1828 and published in English the following year. It already carries many Western characteristics. His subsequent novels appeared in rapid succession from 1833 until 1843. By 1830/31 Sealsfield had returned to Europe, first to Paris, then London, and finally Switzerland, which was to become his third home. During that time he also seems to have been active politically, mostly in the service of the Bonaparte family. Already in the U.S. Sealsfield had become acquainted with exiled Joseph Bonaparte, a brother of Napoleon I of France. Prior to his return to Europe, he had also worked for the *Courrier des Etats Unis*, the paper of the Bonapartist faction in New York.

Much speculation has been given to Sealsfield's political contacts. We know today that he was connected with a number of Jacksonian politicians, including Joel R. Poinsett, first U.S. minister to Mexico and later Secretary of War in the administration of Van Buren. However, much of what has been written on Sealsfield's life including the author's involvement with the Freemasons, is mere conjecture or based on the fictional work—poor sources of biographical information. Obviously, much remains to be clarified concerning the Austrian-American's life, but it is doubtful whether any of it is going to throw more light on his works.

A short stay in the United States from May until October 1837 allowed him a firsthand look at the effects of the economic crisis in the New World. From this time on he became increasingly critical of the United States as a rapidly industrializing country. This development is at odds with his Western, "agrarian" vision of America. It seems that his increasing disillusionment with the New World also contributed to his inability to continue his work as a creative writer. In spite of his great popularity in Germany as well as in the United States, the three-volume *South and North* (1842/43), a novel about Mexico, remains his last completed fictional work.

The final twenty years of his life are relatively uneventful ones. With the exception of a period of five years, which he spent in the United States and during which, at least according to his correspondence, he seems to have busied himself almost exclusively with financial and business transactions, Sealsfield spent the remainder of his life in Switzerland, all the while maintaining his assumed American identity. His correspondence shows that he remained an interested observer of the political as well as literary developments both in Europe and in the United States. In 1846, for example, he ordered two books by the Western prose writer Caroline Kirkland, *A New Home* (1839) and *Western Clearings* (1845), because he was interested in "fresh American impressions." At the same time he watched with bitterness how his Jeffersonian-Jacksonian conceptions of America became less and less significant to a country willing to wage a civil war for what he saw as one-sided economic advantages and, ultimately, the industrialization of the country. However, the aging man, tortured by severe disease, was never quite willing to give up his early vision completely. In his last will, he left part of his property to two young relatives in Moravia in order to facilitate their immigration to the United States. In this way, he hoped that his life's dream would live on in another member of his family—proof of the tenacity with which he himself held on to the ideals of his youth to the very end.

II

After Sealsfield's first novel, *Tokeah; or the White Rose*, had been published by Carey, Lea and Carey in Philadelphia in 1829, various papers and journals speculated on the identity of its author. Due to the Indian theme of the anonymous work, the reviews invariably compared the novel with James Fenimore Cooper's *Leather-Stocking Tales* of which, up to that point, there had been three: *The Pioneers* (1823), *The Last of the Mohicans* (1826), and *The Prairie* (1827). One paper, possibly in a public relations effort, even asked: "Is Mr. Cooper to have a rival, or has a greater than Cooper risen?"

It seems remarkable that an Austrian immigrant, hardly six years in the country, should have been able to master the English (and American) idiom sufficiently not only to publish a novel in English but even to draw public acclaim for his work. Several reviews also stress the *American* quality of *Tokeah* and this is where a discussion of the novel must begin. As the novel's intricate plot is rather closely related to its meaning as a whole, it deserves to be discussed in greater detail here. At first glance, it certainly does invite a comparison with Cooper.

In a stormy December night of the year 1799, a band of Indians, obviously freshly returned from a bloody fight, knock on the door of "Captain John" Copeland's house. Copeland is a backwoodsman and the proprietor of a little inn in the forests of Georgia. The Indian leader, Tokeah, later identified as chief of the Oconee tribe, forces Copeland's wife, a true pioneer woman drawn in the tradition of Ishmael Bush's wife in Cooper's *Prairie*, to assume parental responsibility for a little white girl. After six years, during which Tokeah takes care of the costs for her upbringing but also prevents the Copelands from divulging any news of her existence to the American authorities, the chief comes to make the "White Rose," as she is now called, a member of his tribe. Tokeah, who has repeatedly been tricked and cheated by the whites and who bears a strong hatred against his enemies, wants to leave Georgia and find a new homeland for his tribe in the West, in a place "where no white man has trodden the ground" (Complete Works, 4/I: 38).

Seven years later, the plot is resumed with a description of the small Indian village of the Oconees near Lake Sabine in what is today Texas. Under the guardianship of Canondah, Tokeah's daughter, White Rose has grown to be an attractive teenage girl. In order to counteract American expansion to the West, Tokeah naively hopes to stop white civilization through a series of weddings: Canondah should marry El Sol, a young chief of the powerful tribe of the Cumanchees; White Rose, on the other hand, should become the wife of the "Chief of the Saltlake," the French pirate Lafitte whose true identity and character Tokeah does not realize.

The arrival of Arthur Graham, an English traveler lost in the wilderness, upsets these plans greatly. The aristocratic Graham falls in love with White Rose and enlightens Tokeah as to the true nature of the pirate. The latter, infuriated over the loss of his bride, attacks the Indian village at night. Although the Indians emerge victorious, their losses are heavy and Canondah is killed in the course of the battle. Lafitte is caught and will be brought to a representative of the "Great White Father."

In the meantime, the Englishman's attempt to reestablish contact with white civilization has resulted in his imprisonment in the squatter village of Opelousas, Louisiana. The historical background of the novel is the War of 1812 between the United States and England, and the squatters accuse Graham of espionage and complicity with the Indians. The justice of the peace in Opelousas is John Copeland, who has moved west and become a respectable farmer with political aspirations. The Englishman at first laughs at the idea of imprisonment by American democrats he considers hardly less savage than the Indians, but he is soon convinced by Copeland that his situation is rather serious. Martial law forces Copeland to bring Graham to the military court at the headquarters of Jackson's army.

At about the same time, Tokeah, El Sol, White Rose, and the pirate arrive in Jackson's camp. The Indians confirm Graham's innocence; Copeland becomes reacquainted with his former foster child Rose who, in turn, marries the Englishman a little while later and moves with him to his home in Jamaica. Lafitte manages to escape. Tokeah, who by now has lost his real daughter and his adopted child, returns to his tribe. On the way, he is killed by a band of Indian enemies; thus "he is doomed to die on the land of the whites" (Complete Works, 5/III: 219).

This very sketchy account of a rather intricate plot shows clearly why the reviewers liked to compare *Tokeah* with the *Leather-Stocking Tales*. Just as *The Last of the Mohicans* (1826), Sealsfield's Indian novel deals with the Indian's hopeless fight for survival. Cooper's *Prairie*, published in 1827, may have been even more influential. *The Prairie* is Cooper's only novel with a Western squatter as a central character. In both novels white squatters are pitted against the Indians and in both works the West becomes "the final gathering-place of the redmen" (*The Prairie*, Mohawk Ed. v) and a symbol for the future of white America (in spite of Cooper's idiosyncratic decision to hinder the progress of the Bush family).

Some Sealsfield researchers have interpreted the author's position toward the Indians as one of understanding and benevolence, and identified Sealsfield as an early champion of the interests and rights of the Indian people. This interpretation, however, neglects the literary and historical context of the work. Sealsfield only *appears* to be sensitive towards the Indian cause; historically speaking, one might call this attitude a concession to the primitivistic view of the Indians then held by many readers, especially on the East coast. However, Sealsfield's presentation ultimately favors the westward expansion of the whites as an act of historical necessity.

In a discussion between Tokeah and Jackson late in the novel, the "General" (Jackson), the unacknowledged hero of the novel, explains the white position:

> "Chief," said the general, not without vehemence, "the Great Spirit has made the lands for the white men, and for the red men, that they may live on the fruits which grow on the earth, and dig the soil, and plough the ground; but not for hunting grounds, that some thousands of red men may find deer where millions of people might live peacefully." (Complete Works, 5/III: 162 f.)

This sentence contains the ultimate justification for the white man's actions, outlining a divinely ordained "manifest destiny." God himself has prescribed the victorious march of civilization and agriculture. The Jeffersonian ideal of an agrarian America, carried westward into the new territories of the Louisiana Purchase, becomes a battle-cry against the Indians.

In his book *Savagery and Civilization*, Roy Harvey Pearce has described the nineteenth-century white American attitude towards the Indians as a compromise between the (largely European) primitivistic view of the "noble savage" and the "traditional" anti-Indian positions of American settlers. A mixture of pity and censure is also characteristic of Sealsfield's Indian novel. A certain touch of melancholy does emerge from the text, but it is quickly suppressed and replaced by the celebration of white democracy in North America.

The fate of White Rose among the Indians, as well as the attitude of the narrator concerning this situation, is typical of a number of popular novels of this period. In Catherine M. Sedgwick's *Hope Leslie* (1827), a white girl becomes a member of an Indian tribe, but is severely censured by both her family and the narrator; in Lydia M. Child's *Hobomok* (1824), an American girl is temporarily allowed to marry an Indian, but the author finally manages to restore the actual husband, long believed dead, in order to correct this "humiliation." White Rose, too, cannot remain among the Indian tribe that has saved her, but needs to be "lifted up" to white civilization. Her attraction to the Englishman is not merely sexual but suggests White Rose's "natural" desire for reacceptance into the white world.

Quite in contrast to Cooper's sinister squatters in *The Prairie*, Sealsfield's whites are lovable Western frontiersmen, simple, with a highly authentic American jargon (including an inclination to profanity of which at least one contemporary Eastern critic complained) and very democratically minded. Copeland, for example, has many of Leather-Stocking's more admirable qualities, including a good mastery of his rifle—the narrator once calls him Hawkeye!—and a simple and rustic manner. However, he is no philosopher of nature, but rather a preacher of democracy. Whereas Leather-Stocking shares the Indian's bitterness when he hears the white settler's axe chopping down a tree, the woodmanship of Copeland's squatters rings throughout the forest as a happy sign of the expansion of American democracy.

In turning his back on the whites in quest of the unsettled West, Tokeah shows a remarkable naiveté and an utter lack of historical perspective. The logic of the novel does not permit the Indians an existence independent of the whites. When attempting to put a halt to the westward expansion by allying himself with the pirate,

Tokeah loses his daughter and a large part of his small tribe. His wish to go "where no white man has trodden the ground" is fulfilled in tragic irony. His fate must be seen as paradigmatic for his tribe and the Indian people of North America as a whole.

But Tokeah's death is fictionally balanced by Jackson's elevation. The novel appeared in February 1829, shortly after Jackson had taken office as President. By writing a book set during the War of 1812, Sealsfield directed the reader's attention automatically toward Jackson, the military hero of that war. There are a number of literary allusions to Jackson in this book, only one of which will be discussed here. In Cooper's novel *The Spy* (1821), which brought him national attention, the loyalist British officer Henry Wharton is accused of espionage and sentenced to death by the Americans. It was a well known fictional fact to American readers that a mysterious "Mr. Harper," who assists in Wharton's escape, is George Washington himself. In Sealsfield's *Tokeah*, under the conditions of martial law, Graham is set free by Jackson. Thus Sealsfield attempted to associate Jackson with Washington in the hope that this would lead to some sort of identification of the two in the reader's mind. Also, in the final pages of *The Spy*, a connection is made between the War of Independence and the War of 1812, thus establishing a kind of historical-imaginative nexus, which Sealsfield's novel draws on as well.

Both text and context of the novel are oriented towards the person of Jackson. The egalitarian community of Opelousas in the southwestern state of Louisiana (then clearly a part of the western section of the country) is the work of the great Western democratic mastermind, Jackson. Jackson is not even mentioned in the book by name, but is always referred to as the "General." In many ways, the book ushers in the period of Jacksonian democracy.

In Sealsfield's later novels, we will continue to meet with Western frontiersmen depicted as the cornerstone and the backbone of American democracy. The Indians, however, no longer make an appearance in his fiction. If we understand Sealsfield's whole work as a novelistic cycle, an epic presenting the United States some fifty years after the Declaration of Independence, we notice that he presents the Indians' total subjugation as a fact to be reckoned with in the course of the country's settlement. Sealsfield, however, agreed with Jackson when the latter said on 6 December 1830 in his Annual Presidential Message: "But true philanthropy reconciles the mind to these vicissitudes as it does to the extinction of one generation to make room for another" (quoted by Pearce, *Savagism* 57).

The German version of *Tokeah* was published in Switzerland in 1833 and was titled *Der Legitime und die Republikaner*. Basically, this revised version echoes the tendency of *Tokeah* in a radicalized form. In a letter serving as a kind of introduction, the advantages which the Indians themselves supposedly derive from their "Removal" from their traditional homelands in the East to areas west of the Mississippi are explained. Thus, the novel as a whole is presented in the historical context of an extremely cruel, anti-Indian policy pursued by Jackson.

The "Legitimate" in the novel is, of course, Tokeah, but legitimacy, a term used with regard to the thrones of Europe, is not part of the rhetoric of the republic and it is therefore not surprising that the "Republicans" receive the moral support of the narrator in the end. In the German version of the novel the nobleman, Graham, is replaced by a commoner in the British navy who, in the end, stays on in Opelousas and marries Copeland's daughter Mary. Thus, in the German version, all parts of the narrative return to Opelousas, thereby stressing Copeland's significance as the founder of the democratic settlement.

18

III.

The first American edition of Sealsfield's most famous novel, *The Cabin Book* (German original title: *Das Kajütenbuch*, 1841) is today one of the most sought-for items in the American antiquarian book business. When it appeared in the United States in 1844, it was hailed as giving "a vivid picture of Texas and its society in its early days, and during the war with Mexico" and as depicting "in graphic and brilliant colors the wild scenes and adventures which have been enacted in that rendezvous." Subsequently, it has been counted among the first of many "Texas novels" in American literature—following Timothy Flint's *Francis Berrian* (1826) and Anthony Ganilh's *Mexico vs. Texas* (1838). This fact probably contributed to the demand for the first edition of the novel, without which a collection of Texas literature would remain incomplete.

Sealsfield's interest in the Southwest as well as Mexico may have to do with his personal experience. Not only did he reside in a state of the Old Southwest, Louisiana, but he is also said to have traveled extensively in Mexico and, possibly, the Mexican province of Texas.

However, as there is no conclusive evidence for these suppositions, the reader of the *Cabin Book* and the two novels directly concerned with Mexico, *The Viceroy and the Aristocrats* (1833) and *South and North* (1842/43), might do well to find other explanations for Sealsfield's interest in this region. In this way, other and more relevant clues for the interpretation of these novels might become available.

Obviously the "Texas question" would have to be part of Sealsfield's overriding concern with the westward expansion of the United States. The U.S. government had once issued a formal declaration stating that they had no claims with regard to Texas. However, Americans had continuously attempted to intrude into the

Mexican province since the beginning of the nineteenth century. In the 1820s, Mexico authorized a settlement of Americans under the leadership of Austin which eventually led to a secessionist movement in Texas, then to the creation of an independent state, the "Lone Star Republic," and, finally, to the incorporation of the territory into the United States. Through Texas, then, developments in Mexico had an immediate impact on the United States. A strong Mexico could persist in its domination of Texas and thus effectively check the further fulfillment of the American "manifest destiny."

Moreover, there was Sealsfield's hostility toward Catholicism in any form. While it is probably true, as his biographers have said, that the renegade priest had a special axe to grind with his former affiliation, anti-Catholicism was a mood then prevalent in the whole country. In the East, Catholic monasteries were burnt down, events which the *Cabin Book* registers as expressive of the "just spirit which always guides the American people" (translation from *Kajütenbuch*, Reclam 24). In the Southwest, a strong, aggressive stand against the Spanish Catholic colony of Mexico, independent since 1821, seemed to be called for. In the words of Ray Allen Billington, the historian of the nativist movement, the task was to "save the West from the Pope."

This is the political context of Sealsfield's three Southwestern novels. *The Viceroy and the Aristocrats* deals almost entirely with internal Mexican affairs. The novel is difficult to comprehend even for twentieth-century readers. It is a fine example of "open form" since there is no actual plot and no individual protagonists who are displaying coherent development of character. Rather, the reader is confronted with a conglomerate of confused scenes following one another in rapid sequence. The narrator himself notices this seeming confusion and states towards the close of the first part of the work that he would "not be surprised if our readers would consider the scenes depicted so far as eruptions of a sick mind" (translation from the German *Virey*, Complete Works, 8: 293). Whatever meaning there might be in this novel must be found in the narrator's attitude towards his material.

One very important clue for the reader of the novel is the realization that the narrator is a *persona* in his own right. In the course of his evaluation of the situation in Mexico, especially in authorial comments, he speaks as an American to other Americans. His American mind is the rational result of a natural and healthy social development. Quite in contrast, the situation in Mexico is unclear; there is an aura of darkness reminiscent of the Middle Ages which pervades the whole country as a result of the Catholic domination of the Spanish colonies. As a consequence, the narrative reflects the state of this diseased society in what must seem to the reader the "eruptions of a sick mind."

Whereas the society of the United States progresses continuously along the lines of an improved democracy, especially as a result of the expansion towards the West, Spanish/Catholic domination leads to a denial of the most elementary human rights for the large majority of Mexicans.

The despotic legacy on the whole country is so strong that the narrator does not expect any change as a result of the struggle of the radical anti-Spanish forces. While North America is presented as a mature democratic and republican society, *The Viceroy* suggests only bloodshed and further bloodshed as a result of a violent Mexican revolution, but no actual improvement.

Although the novel was published in 1834, well after the successful Mexican revolution and following the establishment of an independent Mexican republic, Sealsfield decided to concentrate on "Mexico in the Year 1812," as the subtitle indicates, and he refuses

71748

even to mention its successful liberation from Spain.

Gerhard Friesen's excellent analysis of *The Viceroy* as a "panoramic" novel has shown that the "combined effect of these scenes [of the novel] is that of a gigantic drama with an almost inexhaustible cast of characters . . . . They remain anonymous members of the masses which act as a single corporate body . . . " (49). In contrast to the downcast masses, the American narrator and certain enlightened Mexicans are given the chance of an occasional "panoramic" view, encompassing the whole of Mexican society. As a result of these panoramic views, light is brought into the darkness of Mexico and it becomes possible to understand the country's present and future. The Conde de San Iago, an influential Mexican aristocrat strongly allied to U.S. interests, is the head of a moderate opposition party in Mexico who, unlike the guerilleros, will play a positive role in the future development of the country. Thus, he shares the narrator's insight into the internal conditions of Mexico.

It is remarkable, and highly indicative of Sealsfield's "Americanism," that the person who is most loyal to the "Great Republic of the North" is said to have the most positive function in the future history of Mexico. Change, indeed, will come, says the narrator repeatedly, but it will be slow. The people, in any case, are unable to deal with the problems which affect them most. They are depicted as an unfeeling, passive mass, unable to act on their own.

The similarity of *The Viceroy* to a novel such as Timothy Flint's *Francis Berrian* is interesting. Berrian, the first person narrator, is equally characterized by a panoramic view, suggesting correspondingly deep insights. In many American novels dealing with Mexico published in Sealsfield's period, the attitude of the American towards his Mexican subject matter is one of distinctive superiority. In Anthony Ganilh's *Mexico Versus Texas*, for example, the narrator maintains: "There is [in Mexico] an illiberal and fierce opposition against the introduction and spreading of knowledge . . . ; still, the pupil of the national eye is dilating and light is making a rapid progress" (v). Needless to say, the importers of light are Americans.

Some eight or nine years following *The Viceroy*, Sealsfield wrote his last book, another Mexican novel: *South and North* (1842/43). It is more complex than *The Viceroy*. Even the title is ambiguous, as it remains unclear whether it refers to Southern and Northern Mexico or to Mexico and the United States. In the novel four young American travelers experience Mexico, to them a mysterious country which they manage to penetrate more and more deeply, but which at the same time becomes more and more threatening to them: "A dreadful destiny . . . threatening to interfere with the motion of the driving gear of our every-day life, threatening to arrest the wheel of fate, threatening to drive us toward a dark calamitous future, toward a world of battles . . . —we must oppose the secretive plans of violent powers pregnant with perils, we must oppose their daggers lurking in the dark and their lassos, and their thousand tools, oppose them in their own bloodstained country, in the midst of the focus of their power . . . " (translation from *Süden und Norden*, Complete Works, 19: 157 f.). After a long, confusing odyssey it slowly becomes clear that the travelers are toys in the hands of the Catholic Church, which has controlled them throughout their stay in Mexico. Dark intrigues and seductive Mexican women, neither ever completely understood, endanger not only the physical well-being but also the mental sanity of the traveler. The Catholic Church is presented as the ultimate agency of evil, terror, and destruction.

Books containing "disclosures" or "revelations" of evil Catholic practices were common in American literature of that period. From Mary Monk's almost gothic *Awful Disclosures of the Hotel*

Dieu Nunnery of Montreal (1836) to Ellen Lester's anti-Jesuit novel *Stanhope Burleigh: The Jesuits in Our Home* (1855), a variety of genres and themes are represented. *South and North* appeared at one of the highpoints of the anti-Catholic, nativist movement and reflects the increasingly radicalized antagonism quite adequately.

South and North contains an interesting fictional variation on a theme also found in *Francis Berrian.* Berrian always stresses the significance of his rational mind—even in extreme situations he never loses his New England coolness. The American travellers in *South and North,* however, find it impossible to control their Mexican experiences rationally. Their minds fall prey to a mysterious country they have never understood, reminiscent of American fear of (and attraction to) primitive and exotic places such as the South Sea islands in Herman Melville's *Typee* (1846). Among the confusion of the Mexican landscape, Mexican life, and the seductiveness of Mexican women, the travellers experience grave mental problems which continue to plague them after their return to the United States. The warning for Americans, not to willingly subject themselves to the influence of the Catholic power, is obviously part of the intended meaning of the novel; however, many aspects of this complex book have several levels of meaning, and some of these reach deeply into the author's personality.

In the dedication of *Mexico Versus Texas,* Anthony Ganilh writes to Samuel Houston that "Texas may be considered as leading a crusade in behalf of modern civilization, against antiquated prejudices and narrow policy of the middle ages, which still govern the Mexican republic" (iii). This dedication might well be said to be one of the *leitmotifs* of Sealsfield's best-known work, *The Cabin Book.* A novel consisting of five different parts or stories told at a dinner party of Southern planters at Natchez, the book certainly breathes the atmosphere of American enlightenment in its later—

Jacksonian—version. The first two parts cover the liberation of Texas. In the fictional history of one Edward N. Morse, settler in Texas and eventually General in the Texan army, "public history" is reflected in the fictional experience of one man. In the course of the Texan struggle for independence, in more than one sense a re-enactment of the American War of Independence, Morse becomes a new, "regenerated" individual, whose character is presented as exemplary for established Americans. In the book, these Americans are represented by twenty-four planters, the audience for the narrator's stories. They have lost the original American revolutionary spirit and given up on their democratic ideals. Partly, they have even become financiers and speculators. Thus Texas is actually needed in order to reform the American character and to inspire the country's return to the original values of the founding fathers.

Morse's regeneration, to summarize a small part of the plot, takes place as a result of a highly personal religious experience after he had lost his way in the prairies of Texas. He is saved by a criminal named Bob Rock, a murderer whom God had placed in Texas in order to demonstrate that under the extreme conditions of a frontier state such as Texas, even criminals may perform a positive and useful social function. Thus Morse is forced to learn that life on the Western frontier requires a value system different from that in the established states of the East. Following his dramatic rescue, he meets with a Texas justice of the peace. This man convinces him of the truth of the Western interpretation of Rock's life and provides a sociopolitical, even philosophical introduction to life in the West: "In the prairie . . . a different light starts shining inside you than in your big cities; after all, your cities are constructed by humans, are polluted by human breath; the prairie, however, is made by God; there life is given by His pure breath" (translation from *Ka-*

jütenbuch, Reclam 120).

The justice of the peace, a committed Jeffersonian, finally convinces Morse to enlist in the Texan army. Morse is now ready to take this step—as a regenerated human being he enters the Texan fight for independence.

The other stories told among the planters that evening concern Ireland and the Latin-American struggle for independence from Spain. Altogether, *The Cabin Book*, which appeared in numerous editions in German and in at least two English translations, is a "Western" with global dimensions. Starting from the westward expansion into Texas, a familiar pattern in Sealsfield's novels, it reaches out into the world, suggesting that the values of the American West will bring about global regeneration. By the same token, America's "innocence," as it still appeared in *Tokeah* and other works yet to be discussed, is over. The very necessity to reach out to Texas in order to reenact the drama of the American Revolution, designed to have a cathartic effect on American society, shows that much has changed in America and Sealsfield's perception of it.

IV.

Much has been said so far about Sealsfield's Western vision of society. In *Tokeah*, Indian culture was to be replaced by a white civilization growing out of the frontier experience; in the Mexico and Texas novels, the establishment of a distinctly Western society in Texas had the task to both check the advance of the un-American, Catholic forces and to inspire established America with its old, revolutionary values.

However, little has as yet been said to specify the character of that Western society. In the period of Jacksonian democracy, Western ideas and ideals were embodied in myths and symbols—in literature as well as in everyday political life, in newspapers, and in election campaigns. The portrayal of a Western society was thus a highly imaginative task and has as much, if not more, to do with the mythic levels of the people's *mind* as it did with the actualities of life on the frontier.

When Sealsfield's *Life in the New World* was advertised in the *New World* magazine in 1844, the ad read as follows:

> When crossing the Fulton Ferry the other day, we happened to be seated in the cabin opposite to a gray-haired man, who rested on his rifle and had a couple of dogs crouching at his feet. It was evidently an old hunter. His iron-frame had probably weathered more than sixty winters; yet his joints appeared to be as firmly knit together and his muscles to be as full of strength as they had ever been. He was reading a pamphlet with a light-green cover. We looked—it was Seatsfield [sic]? . . . Feeling interested, we made bold to ask the old man what he thought of that book.
>
> "Sir," said he, "next to the Bible, it's the most faithful book I ever met with. I was a trapper in my young days, and I have hunted on the banks on the Red River. Nobody ever understood the West better than this man Seatsfield. By jingo, sir, it makes my blood run faster to read this." (*New World* 18 May 1844, 621)

It is highly doubtful whether the reporter of the *New World*, incidentally also the publishing house of "Seatsfield's" works in translation, actually met a Western hunter with his two dogs and a rifle on the Fulton Ferry reading Sealsfield. Rather, it appears as though the author of these lines makes use of the same imaginative *conceptions* of the West as most Western writers, including Sealsfield, did. Sealsfield's fictional writing is proven truthful through the old man's memory of the West. To the old hunter, Sealsfield's book is almost as *faithful* as the Bible, i.e., it becomes something the old man believes in or wants to believe in. Nobody ever *understood* the West better than Sealsfield, says the old man—such an understanding does not require a "realistic" portrayal but an imaginative presentation of the "spirit" of the West, faithful also with regard to beliefs, conventions, and clichés.

Sealsfield's longest work, a cycle of five novels, is central to his *oeuvre* and central to his understanding and imaginative use of the West. In America, the book appeared in 1844 under the title of *Life in the New World*. The literal translation of the original German title published between 1834 and 1837 is "Portraits of Life in the Western Hemisphere"—referring to both America as the Western continent and the Western states or territories as opposed to the American East.

The five parts of the cycle have a common first person narrator, the young Louisiana planter George Howard. We first encounter Howard in New York City looking for a suitable wife. However, he seems a rather confused individual: "Who," he asks himself, "in this mad New-York, this merry American Paris, could come to sober thoughts?" (*Life in the New World*, 1844: 9). He soon sees through the shallowness of life in the East and recognizes that personal relationships and love are always expressed in terms of money in New York. Disgusted he leaves the East and starts out on a journey West in space, time, and spirit. We learn that he is the son of a respectable Virginia planter who had emigrated to Louisiana some time ago to start afresh the way "even the Jeffersons and Washingtons have begun. And happy will it be for us if future generations do not view this way of renovating [rejuvenating] society as too loathsome!" (40 f.).

However, Howard has not yet adopted the true Western spirit, else he would not have gone to the East in search of a spouse. He wants to play the role of an "absentee-gentleman" (50): reap the profits from his farm without actually living on the land and leading the life of a farmer. Thus, the five parts of the book in a way depict the "Education of George Howard." In the course of his voyage in space and time, Howard—along with the reader—encounters all segments of Western and especially Southwestern society and also learns to understand and appreciate its historical growth.

In its dynamic character, the process of moving farther and farther West makes the reader participate in this voyage in the very act of reading, and it is in this sense that Sealsfield dedicated "To the German Nation . . . these pictures of the domestic and public life of the Free Citizens of a Free State, destined to historical greatness . . . as a mirror for self-examination" (Dedication to *Life in the New World*). Dynamic "pictures" of the country pass by the eye of the reader in an almost cinematic way, thereby not only informing Sealsfield's audience about the new country and especially the West, but also attempting to find a formal equivalent to the ongoing expansion towards the West.

In the course of the five parts of the work, various narrators present narrations of their own, which all become part of Howard's overall narrative. Critics have accused Sealsfield of making his books unnecessarily complicated due to this complex structure of naratives within the original narrative, but they have overlooked the fact that this structural device has its equivalent in American literature—Sealsfield was doing nothing less than making the Western storyteller the structural device of his novels!

Thus it is not surprising that many of the characters we meet in Sealsfield's books come directly out of well-known American tall-tales. One of the chief archetypal Western characters in the history of the American imagination is Daniel Boone, the "patriarch of Kentucky," the man who, in his old age, left Kentucky for Missouri because the population density of ten per square mile was too crowded for him (cf. Cooper, *The Prairie*, Mohawk Ed. 3). Ever since John Filson's *The Discovery, Settlement and Present State of Kentucke* (1784!) appeared with an appendix titled "The Adventures of Col. Daniel Boon; containing a Narrative of the Wars of Kentucke," Boone had been shown in the typical posture of a hardy Westerner, simple but shrewd, individualistic but democratic, oriented towards achievement but egalitarian. A number of literary presentations of Boone's life by such authors as Flint and Hall precede Sealsfield's Westerners who are obviously modeled after these examples.

Boone and Boone-like characters as well as their creators face a dilemma which is difficult to solve. On the one hand, they are at home in the wilderness, love to be alone and commune with untouched nature, very much like Cooper's Leather-Stocking. On the other hand—quite in contrast to Leather-Stocking—these men are also conscious agents of progress and white civilization. Their very struggle on the frontier prepares for the advance of civilization from which they are moving away. In part five of *Life in the New World*, titled "Nathan, the Squatter-Regulator," Sealsfield has the patriarch of Louisiana, Nathan Strong, who has singlehandedly fought whole European armies and conquered the wilderness, move on to Texas because he does not want to subject himself to the restraints of civilization.

Ultimately, this fictional dilemma, which echoes Boone's removal to Missouri, as described, for example, in Timothy Flint's *Bio-graphical Memoir of Daniel Boone* (1833), stems from a theoretical problem which is part of American expansionist ideology. The "regeneration" of Europeans, Europeanized (Eastern) Americans, and other non-Westerners was going to be a result of man's life on the frontier, his active interaction with the wilderness. Just as Frederick Jackson Turner would formulate it in his later "Thesis," breathing the very spirit we find in early Western fiction, the "new" American was explained as a result of the conditions of life on the outer edge of civilization.

Ironically, however, the frontier would sooner or later lose its wilderness quality and cease to be frontier precisely as a result of the work of the pioneers. Thus, new droves of Americans would be forced to move even farther west, into Texas, beyond Texas, and finally to the Pacific region. A permanent movement towards the West would be the only way to keep Jefferson's rural utopia intact, but even while the country was expanding towards the West with breathtaking rapidity, the inevitable end of this process could be foreseen.

Nevertheless, while it worked, the desire to "conquer" ever new frontiers provided an excellent imaginative vehicle for the political aspirations of the United States. Ideally, the true American citizen had to fight two types of "barbarism": that of the East (Europeans, monarchies, aristocratic societies) and that of the West (Indians, wilderness, and wild beasts). In between lay the historically short-lived Jacksonian America: an existence somewhere in between pioneer and farmer, simple and comfortable, rough but "civilized."

This imaginary model which can be found in many literary and non-literary documents of the Jacksonian era, lies at the heart of Sealsfield's writings. In *Life in the New World* he comes close to spelling out the formula theoretically, but he usually attempts to keep to the imaginative narrative, to the presentation of images and scenes.

Shortly after leaving New York, Howard finds himself lost in the backwoods on the banks of the Tennessee. After a long period of wandering through the wilderness, he finds quarters in a small community which is in the midst of a local election campaign. The presentation of the small settlement of Bainbridge, Alabama, following the account of Howard's life in New York City, has a specific function. In one sense, the "electioneering" discloses the essential simplicity of the backwoods character. There is a tall tale-like quality when Bob Shags, one of the candidates, strongly protests American aid to the Greeks, whom he mistakes for Creek Indians, or when he takes the "general tariff" (to which the West was opposed) to be a real-live General—"one of the wildest aristocrats that ever lived" (21). At the same time, however, the simplicity of this primitive but egalitarian democratic environment seems far superior to the manners of the moneyed "mushroom aristocracy" in New York.

As Sealsfield himself had published this section of *Life in the New World* a few years earlier in the *New-York Mirror*, we have to assume that it was his original creation, possibly inspired by actual experience. On other occasions, however, Sealsfield liked to use traditional examples of American humor such as the incident involving a Yankee peddler from Connecticut named Jared Bundle.

The Yankee peddler who wants to trick Southerners and Westerners is, of course, a stock character in American humor. This particular episode was taken from William Gilmore Simms' border romance *Guy Rivers: A Tale of Georgia* (1834), in which a Jared Bunce tricks a group of gold miners. Sealsfield makes use of Simms' material in order to present the *locale* of his novel, the ever-dynamic Southwest. In such a heterogeneous and constantly shifting society—quite appropriately the scene takes place on a steamboat—the most common cultural denominator of frontier people and established planters, trappers and merchants, is humor. American humor, especially as emerging from tall tales, has a specifically egalitarian function in Sealsfield's works as well as in American Western literature as a whole.

Sealsfield makes use of a great number of American literary sources. Chapter III of Part One, for example, titled "The Kidnapper," is modeled after Timothy Flint's "The Lost Child." It portrays—even more so than Flint's story with its religious didacticism—solidarity in Western society. The kidnapping of the son of an only modestly affluent backwoods farmer becomes the concern of *all* citizens, because the questions of individual freedom and the safety of private property depend on it. The chapter is a good example of a highly idealized version of an egalitarian society where individual wealth and interests do not supersede the interest of the "public good."

The general tendency of Sealsfield's works is egalitarian, culturally as well as socially. There is, in view of the superiority of the white settlers, no place for an Indian culture separate from white civilization. Catholic opposition, with all its hierarchies so grossly suspicious to Americans, cannot be permitted to persist. Mexico is inferior when compared to the United States, in need of "enlightenment"—hence the justified annexation of Texas. Socially, Sealsfield's Western society provides for a massively egalitarian perspective, due to the equalizing effect of the frontier: "Thus, with us [observes Howard], the points of social positions touch each other; and, by continual contact, smooth each other's harsh and rough corners. The son of a senator builds his hut on a piece of woodland, which joins the property of a Scotch drover, whose wife was probably the servant of the senator's daughter, who now meets her as a friendly neighbor, and returns every little civility with equal obligations. Thus necessity promotes with us, to a certain degree, that social republican system . . . " (*Life in the New World* 102).

There was, however, one significant flaw in this egalitarian picture which had already bothered some of the Founding Fathers and which worried Sealsfield's liberal-minded European audience. Writing as he did about the Southwest and Louisiana, Sealsfield had to account especially for that defect. Many of the Founding Fathers felt rather worried about the establishment of a democratic Republic based on egalitarian principles which did not even mention the emancipation of the slaves. While many Northerners, and also Southerners like Jefferson (whose ambivalent attitude towards the topic has acquired biographical notoriety), worried about this problem, the general view held in the South was that the question of slavery had nothing to do with egalitarian principles. Probably one of the most extreme explanations was furnished by Calhoun, who believed firmly that, as in ancient Greece, democracy virtually depended on the continued existence of slavery.

Sealsfield, probably a slaveholder himself for a short period, firmly believed that slavery as an institution was to be defended in the interest of all parties concerned. It would be wrong, as some critics have done, to let his pro-slavery views invalidate his otherwise egalitarian philosophy. Indeed, Jackson himself was a slaveholder and, despite his populist rhetoric, certainly no advocate of an immediate or even gradual emancipation.

Two of the five volumes of *Life in the New World* deal with the topic of slavery. At that time the topic was a hot one in the United States. Since the beginning of the 1830s, the abolitionists had increased their agitation in the North; and since 1831, white Southern readers could actually find their favorite nightmare printed up in a book: *The Confessions of Nat Turner*, the account of one of the bloodiest slave rebellions in the history of the South.

Sealsfield, who made use of Turner's insurrection in *Life in the New World*, shared fully the anxieties of the South. In order to patch up certain inconsistencies, he even went so far as to misrepresent his favorite, Jefferson. When Jefferson had written in his *Notes on the State of Virginia* (1784) "Indeed I tremble for my country when I reflect that God is just; that his justice cannot sleep forever; that considering numbers, nature and the natural means only, a revolution of the wheel of fortune, an exchange of situation is among possible events . . . " (Torchbook Ed., 1964: 156), he spoke of America's black slaves. When Sealsfield used it in order to preface the German edition of *Tokeah*, he inferred, although he must have known better, that Jefferson was concerned with the Indians.

The logic of his novel suggests an inclination towards the "positive good theory" of slavery which demanded not apologies but the defense of slavery as a morally positive institution. Parts of his *Life in the New World* read like a plantation novel. The slaves are presented as ignorant children who need their "massa" and "maum" in order to stay alive and happy. The view of the plantation as an organic community and a happy familial entity had been extremely common in Southern thinking since the 1830s. Many stock characters of the later plantation literature tradition derive from this early period in which Sealsfield had a part.

Ultimately, however, the Austrian-American monk, whose secret ill-feeling concerning the topic of slavery can be gathered from a number of contradictory tendencies in his novels, seems to have been able to rationalize the divergency between Western egalitarianism and the interests of the Southern planters' aristocracy only through his overriding belief in America's manifest destiny.

George Howard is a rather curious character, unsure of himself and generally not at all amiable. He is totally split between his great principles as an American and democrat—which he shares with Jackson—and his fear of a possible emancipation of the slaves. While he is certain that Northern capitalism would exploit blacks in worse ways than Southern slavery, he continuously searches for new rationalizations and justifications. In the end, the long narrative in Part Five concerning Nathan and the initial American settlement of Louisiana suggests clearly that this state could never have been won for white civilization without the work of black slaves; adverse factors such as extreme forms of vegetation and climate would have been too strong. At that point, which practically coincides with the conclusion of the cycle and which brings about the desired harmony between Western frontiersman and Southern planter, humanitarian considerations are no longer important.

The overriding task remains the necessity to fulfill America's manifest destiny and to win Louisiana for white, Protestant Americans (Nathan's settlement in Louisiana took place prior to the Louisiana purchase in 1803).

Sealsfield's fictional model of a Western egalitarian society, a model which approaches a political program, becomes thereby coherent and complete. The time of the action of *Life in the New World* coincides with the beginnings of the Jacksonian period; throughout the cycle, there are references to Jackson and a new era of American politics.

Chronologically and geographically, the *Cabin Book* would be the logical continuation of the cycle just discussed. Already, Nathan, who is mentioned in passing in the *Cabin Book*, has made inroads into Texas and prepared the American takeover of that territory. Half of Sealsfield's fictional America is already under white Anglo-Saxon control. Did he feel that his highly dynamic model was limited, that the American West was not infinite?

V.

On at least two occasions Sealsfield attempted to move away from his primary concern with the American West and investigated the possibilities of a fictional presentation of the East as well as Europe, thus anticipating later American authors' attempt to define American identity by contrasting the New World with the Old. The earlier of these two attempts was *Morton, or the Grand Tour* (1835), a book which never appeared in English. As its title implies, this novel reaches over to Europe in an attempt to give Sealsfield's fictional world global dimensions.

Although it can hardly be compared with Faulkner's Yoknapatawpha County, we may indeed speak of Sealsfield's fictional world since he allows some of his characters to appear or to be mentioned in several novels. As we can gather from a small remark made in *Life in the New World*, Morton is a friend of George Howard. In contrast to Howard, however, Morton has chosen a different route. Disillusioned through the loss of his wealth as a result of reckless trading, Morton is driven to the brink of suicide. Almost ready to terminate his life, he is saved by one of the ideal representatives of the Sealsfieldian world, Colonel Isling, an old Pennsylvania German and veteran of the Revolutionary War. The understanding old man convinces Morton that he has a special responsibility to his country, since he is a descendant of a family of historical significance to America (his great-uncle, for example, is hinted to be Thomas Jefferson). Isling offers Morton a loan to enable him to start a plantation on the Mississippi which would make him a wealthy man within four years. Morton, however, decides to accept an offer by a Philadelphia banker and financier, Stephen Girard, a historical figure. Girard sends him to Europe where he soon becomes enmeshed in confusing situations and, so at least it seems, entrapped in the net of international finance.

Critics have attempted to show that Sealsfield's own experience lies at the heart of the novel. The presentation of Morton as Stephen Girard's ambassador to Europe as well as his relationship with the

37

mysterious London-based financier Lomond (a character taken from a novella by Balzac) may have inspired critics to detect a reflection of Sealsfield's mysterious life in these parts of the novel. However, the mystery of Sealsfield's life or rather our scarce knowledge of factual information does not justify the filling of biographical gaps with fiction.

Morton is Sealsfield's attempt to create a fictional portrait of the East and of Europe. A champion of agriculture (just as Colonel Isling at the beginning of the novel), Sealsfield agreed with Jefferson on the negative influence of urban centers on human and social life: "The mobs of great cities add just so much to the support of pure government as sores do to the strength of the human body" (Jefferson, *Notes* 159). According to this view, urban areas in Europe as well as in the United States are the centers of destructive finance and, at the same time, of poverty in the wake of beginning industrialization. Morton clearly makes the wrong decision when he decides against the well-meant advice and help of Sealsfield's ideal American, Colonel Isling. Whether the author meant to educate the young American through an extended European experience or whether he meant to let him perish unredeemed is not the point: Sealsfield was obviously unable to complete *Morton* just as he had failed to complete a second work dealing, at least in part, with Europe. Clearly, Morton is an outsider to the European financial oligarchy and his feeling of confusion as well as the generally confusing plot of the novel must be attributed to the narrator's negative feeling toward the society he describes.

The second work in which Sealsfield attempted to deal with urban life remained equally incomplete. If *Life in the New World* is a fictional portrait of the beginnings of the Jacksonian period and oriented towards the West, *Rambleton*, first published in German in 1839/40, was written under the impression of the financial and economic crisis of 1837. Judging from those parts which were published, *Rambleton* was possibly Sealsfield's most ambitious project. The German title, *Deutsch-Amerikanische Wahlverwandt-schaften* (*German-American Elective Affinities*) refers to Goethe's novel *The Elective Affinities* (1809). The concept of the "elective affinities" implies a special relationship between German-speaking Europeans and Americans and it is probable that in this novel, the European-American writer attempted to do justice to his mixed heritage.

Rambleton consists of several parts which, unlike in the case of the earlier *Life in the New World*, are integrally connected with each other. It is not a novelistic cycle, designed to show America's progressive advance towards the West, but an attempt at a fictional entity trying to present the "natural" kinship between two "new nations," the United States and Germany.

In a fragmented version the political context of the work appears in the text itself. The problems of the time most prominently discussed concern the increase of paper money, President Van Buren's refusal to comply with demands brought forward by influential speculators, and the economic disaster in the wake of many business failures threatening the economy of the whole country.

However, these problems are not elaborated on but only mentioned in passing or implied in observations, dialogues, meetings, etc. The street gangs of both parties—the "Whigs" and the radically democratic "Locofocos"—fight bitter battles and there is an increasing degree of social polarization. The financial aristocracy despises the democratic traditions and the mob completely disregards constitutional and democratic rules.

Mr. Ramble, a nouveau-riche financier, is the representative of the financial oligarchy. His rapid career has not ruined his monetary instinct but it has had a permanently negative effect on his emotional life. His daughter, Dougaldine, and Erwin Dish, her evil "fashionable" cousin, are also part of this negatively drawn urban society.

Acreshouse in Upstate New York, the home of the conservative Rambleton family, forms a natural contrast to the degenerate life in the city. The Rambletons have remained faithful to their American tradition. They stress the significance of agriculture and of rural life in general and refuse to enter into reckless and uncertain financial speculations. In *Rambleton*, the "progressive" West can no longer serve as positive anti-type to urban life but is replaced by the tradition-oriented farm existence in the rural parts of New York State. The literary "West" is thus shown to be a mythic place, a mental condition rather than a geographical place at a certain historical moment.

"Progressive" for the misguided younger generation in *Rambleton* no longer connotes the utopian belief in an ideal American democracy which was typical for the Western novels. The central concern of those living in urban centers is "fashion"—recently imported from Europe.

Erwin Dish, for example, has only ridicule left for democracy and American institutions as he feels that monarchies are again the order of the day. Even Harry Rambleton, educated in the conservative-democratic tradition, is not safe from the influence of this young financier. For a period, he, too, joins the "fashionables" in Saratoga Springs, the New York spa preferred by the city's elite. There he falls in love with the "Queen of Fashion," Dougaldine, who has known him and his family from early childhood. However, he cannot reveal his true identity and his rural origin, for fear of losing her. When Dougaldine, who has had secret misgivings about her role as a queen of fashion for some time, finds she has been tricked

40

by Rambleton, she refuses to marry him. Instead, she encourages the efforts of her cousin Erwin Dish until, without her knowing, the general public regards her as his fiancée.

When her father, outraged over her social and financial escapades, demands an immediate marriage to Erwin, she escapes the threatening confusion of city life and takes refuge with the Rambletons in the countryside. As a result of the general economic chaos, Dougaldine's father goes bankrupt.

This short account of parts of the plot (which does not do justice to the work as a whole) clearly shows that *Rambleton* has a special quality when compared to the Western novels. In the latter, the basic mood was positive and optimistic, in *Rambleton* bitter irony dominates the text.

At some point, Sealsfield seems to have recognized that he was unable to bring the work to a satisfactory conclusion. Although it is suggested that Dougaldine has fallen in love again, this time with a German baron, the discrepancies and contradictions so far outlined in the text seem to be too great to make possible a harmonious ending similar to that of *Life in the New World* .

The special German-American relationship, suggested by the concept of the "Wahlverwandtschaft," certainly no light matter for the Austrian-American author, is expressed in a series of misunderstandings rather than in a special form of transatlantic companionship. Thus, the "Wahlverwandtschaften" between Germany/Europe and the United States exist on a rudimentary level at best—after all what sort of a special relationship was there for a democratically minded author to portray, that of the German baron with the New York belle, of European aristocracy and American noveau-riche?

Rambleton will require closer observation and analysis by future critics, less in view of Sealsfield's decreasing enthusiasm about

American democracy per se (as some critics have held) than as a curious critique of developing capitalism and industrialization which the author considered to be "backwards" and "European." Obviously, Sealsfield did not realize how conservative his own position, seemingly the vanguard in 1829, had become by the close of the 1830s.

Sealsfield as a man and as a novelist seems to have clung tenaciously to his original ideals right to the end of his creative period and, as his correspondence shows, to the end of his life. His times changed and he was forced to react, but when he attempted to deal with new social developments which did not fit his world view and which he disliked, he failed as a novelist. Ironically, his view of America as a highly dynamic society was in itself static.

He repeatedly attempted to work on other novelistic projects which we know about through his correspondence. Whether they were even half-way completed or not, Sealsfield decided not to release them for publication. He was a very productive writer as long as he found his work relevant to the time and the audience for which he wrote. When he attempted to continue writing at a time when he felt history was passing him by, he could no longer devise aesthetic solutions to problems he no longer wanted to face.

VI.

Are we really justified in calling Sealsfield a Western American writer? Most of the novels discussed here were published in Germany or Switzerland first and translated into English only some years later. Although Sealsfield spent a good deal of time in the United States, he was, after all, born in Austria and did not get to the New World until he was thirty years of age. Finally, one might point out his well-established position in nineteenth-century German and Austrian literature and the many studies that have been done of Sealsfield's works in the context of European cultural and literary history and wonder how Sealsfield could be both a European *and* an American writer.

Earlier in this study, I focused primarily on Sealsfield's works and their kinship to Western American literature and thought. By comparing these works with other American literary productions of the same period, by demonstrating sources and influences on Sealsfield's works and by studying the intellectual and historical context of the 1820s and 1830s, I have attempted to establish Sealsfield's "Americanness" on the basis of his works and their meaning to American readers. Sealsfield must be regarded as an Austrian-American writer who, although he was raised in one culture, at some point adopted important and major segments of the culture and even the way of thinking of his host country.

Sealsfield was a political refugee belonging to the group of anti-absolutistic liberals who had emigrated from Austria and Germany since the beginning of the 1820s. Different from most exiles who had settled in various European countries, Sealsfield did not expect a speedy return to his homeland. His commitment to his new country, coupled with an extraordinary talent, enabled him to gain a degree of intercultural competence which allowed him to go back and forth between the German and the English languages as well as between European and American cultures.

For quite a while, the study of American literature, focusing on literature written in English, neglected the works written by first or second generation immigrants, although one might say that such works are in many ways at the very heart of the American experience. The increasing interest in what has become known as ethnic literature in recent years, however, requires that more attention be given to such writers as Sealsfield. This is especially important in the case of an immigrant writer who was aware of the "mainstream" American literature of his period and who creatively reworked this American tradition into his own fiction.

Another important aspect which requires Sealsfield's consideration as an American author is his reception in the United States. Different from many immigrant writers who are known only to a small segment of American society, Sealsfield was, for a short period, a very well-known figure in American literature.

In a diary entry, Longfellow called the Austrian-American writer "our favorite Sealsfield," and it has indeed been shown that Sealsfield's *Life in the New World* has had a significant influence on parts of *Evangeline* (1847). What Longfellow liked in Sealsfield's works was the presentation of the Western landscape and Western life; he obviously appreciated him as a Western writer.

In his sketch "A Select Party," which forms part of the collection of works titled *Mosses from an Old Manse* (1846), Hawthorne, discussing the state of American literature at the time, makes an ironic comment with regard to the "celebrated Seatsfield." While this remark suggests that Sealsfield was no favorite of Hawthorne, it also testifies to the renown Sealsfield enjoyed in and around the year 1844 in the United States.

Edgar Allan Poe, always ready to defend American literature from the point of view of literary nationalism, attacked Sealsfield repeatedly and thereby documented indirectly Sealsfield's prominence on the American literary scene.

How did Sealsfield become so well-known in the New World? Only his first novel, *Tokeah*, was originally written in English; it was published anonymously in Philadelphia under the supervision of the author himself. Although this book received a series of good reviews, it did not create Sealsfield's later fame in the United States.

44

Starting in the 1830s, Sealsfield's German-language novels were rather successful in Europe. For the European, especially the German audience, the mere mention of America served to inspire critical anti-absolutist and liberal minds. In view of the strict censorship exerted by Metternich and his subordinates, direct criticism of socio-political conditions in Germany and Austria was impossible—even in the form of fiction. Thus, instead of criticizing life in their own country, an increasing number of European writers wrote about *other* countries which could serve as yardsticks for the evaluation of one's own country—by implication. A novel on America could therefore be used as an effective tool of criticism against which the censors were powerless. Some writers even wrote "America novels" without ever having been to the New World.

Among these writers, Sealsfield occupies a special position, because his books could be appreciated not only by a European audience intent on learning about the development of the trans-atlantic republic but also by American readers. Americans, of course, were interested in his writings not only because they reflect the same American "spirit" which Sealsfield had come to know in the United States two decades earlier but also because of the flattering nature of Sealsfield's depiction of the United States.

By the mid-1840s, the time when Sealsfield's works became famous in the United States, the interest in the frontier was still as strong as it had been in the 1820s, and, because it was further removed, had an even greater appeal to the American imagination. The spirit of literary nationalism rings through the lines of the *New World*, advertising the works of Sealsfield, "the great and popular author": "Our mountains—rivers—cataracts—ocean lakes—forests, all the magnificent natural features of this mighty land, are described with the most remarkable spirit and truth" (*New World* 4 May 1844, 572). The Texas issue was one of the most widely discussed questions in the country and the anti-Catholic feeling reached one of its highpoints in 1844 with the Philadelphia riots.

Thus, it was not surprising that the businessmen at Winchester's New World Press, the publishers of the *New World*, expected to reap high profits from an English edition of Sealsfield's works. It was the time prior to the introduction of an International Copyright and therefore cheaper to reprint (and translate) European authors than to pay royalties to American writers. While reprinting European authors such as Balzac or Dickens could be highly profitable, American publishers "pirating" foreign authors were always vulnerable to the charge that they were unpatriotic since the reprinted works usually dealt with non-American topics written by foreigners. Sealsfield's writings, however, offered the possibility of publishing what they called "genuinely" American works without paying extra royalties. Suddenly Winchester, one of the most important American pirates, could present himself as a supporter of American literature, as a man who would make sure that these "true pictures of American society and life" would "find their way into every family in the land" (*New World* 4 May 1844, 572).

This complex situation also explains the scorn on the part of Hawthorne and Poe. Previously, American writers, while they were at a natural disadvantage when compared with the cheaper, pirated editions of Europeans, could at least point to their American subject matter. Sealsfield's novels, however, intruded into their very own creative domain and diminished their chances on the American market.

Winchester translated and published most of Sealsfield's works in cheap installments priced at 12.5 cents each. This edition caused considerable excitement in the United States, especially as Sealsfield appeared to be an American writer who had received recognition in Europe before even his name had become known in the United States.

Sealsfield himself seems to have had no knowledge of the pirated editions of his work at first. He mentioned the great success of his work which was "in the hands not just of thousands but hundreds of thousands of citizens of the United States" in 1845 (translation from *Legitime*, Complete Ed., 6: xi). Later on, however, he sharply criticized the American pirates, these "leeches and torturers of all authors" who misspelled his assumed name as "Seatsfield" (letter, 25 April 1854).

Already one year earlier, in 1843, *Blackwood's Edinburgh Magazine* had translated parts of Sealsfield's works for the British audience. At the time, *Blackwood's* was a magazine of considerable renown and Winchester lost no time in issuing a pirated edition as soon as the original reached American shores. Thus, Winchester had, probably totally ignorant of the fact at first, actually printed two different versions of Sealsfield's writings, both of which received considerable attention in the United States.

As Sealsfield's works did not continue to enjoy the popularity they had upon their first appearance, much of the attention bestowed on his novels was probably due to Winchester's sensationalist marketing techniques. However, some works, notably the *Cabin Book*, continued to be reprinted in the United States until the 1880s. There can be no doubt that Sealsfield appealed to a large number of American readers who were fascinated with his imaginative rendering of the American West and Southwest. By 1844, much of Western literature was still in its infancy and Sealsfield was regarded as a pioneer of the literary West, along with such writers as Timothy Flint, James Hall, James Kirke Paulding, William Gilmore Simms, and others.

Modern readers, aware of subsequent Western writing, will be able to place Sealsfield at the very beginning of American literature. While much of later Western American literature is more sophisticated, more refined and, at times, very different in outlook, we can observe the emergence of an early fictional West in Sealsfield's work. In their insistence on a Western "mission" on a global scale, his works are fascinating to the modern mind which has become accustomed to America's global significance: "It seems as if they [the Americans] were destined, by Providence, like the birds of passage, to convey the seeds of freedom throughout the world, which their example has greatly contributed to plant in so large a part of it" (*Tokeah*, Complete Works, 4/I: 180 f.). In light of the appeal much of Sealsfield's work makes to the modern mind and in recognition of his significance to American literary history—both as a Western American and an Austrian-American writer—Sealsfield's works should be "rediscovered" and reclaimed for American literature.

Selected Bibliography

The publication history of Sealsfield's novels is very complex and includes a great number of editions in many languages. Among the German editions, only the most recent editions which are available on the market will be listed. The most important English translations of Sealsfield's works will also be listed. An asterisk indicates an edition quoted in this study.

WORKS BY SEALSFIELD

A. BOOKS

Sämliche Werke [Complete Works], edited by Karl J. R. Arndt *et al.* Hildesheim, N.Y.: Olms, 1972 ff. Twenty-nine volumes are planned; so far, twenty-three have been published. The years given for each title indicate the year of the original publication and the year of the publication in the reprint edition by Olms.

Vol. 1: C. Sidons, *Die Vereinigten Staaten von Nordamerika, nach ihrem politischen, religioesen und gesellschaftlichen Verhaeltnisse betrachtet*, 1827; 1972.

*Vol. 2: *The United States of North America as they are. The Americans as they are*, 1827 f.; 1972; slightly revised version of the German work published as vol. 1 of the *Complete Works*.

Vol. 3: *Austria as It Is: or Sketches of Continental Courts*, 1828, contains also the German translation by V. Klarwill, published in 1919: *Österreich, wie es ist*; 1972.

*Vol. 4/5: *The Indian Chief; or, Tokeah and the White Rose*, 1829; 1972. The 1829 edition was published by Carey, Lea & Carey, Philadelphia.

*Vol. 6/7: *Der Legitime und die Republikaner. Eine Geschichte aus dem letzten englischen-amerikanischen Kriege* [The Legitimate and the Republicans. A Story from the last Anglo-American War], 1833; 1973.

Vol. 8/9: *Der Virey und die Aristokraten oder Mexico im Jahre 1812* [The Viceroy and the Aristocrats or Mexico in the Year 1812], 1833; 1974.

Vol. 10: *Morton oder die große Tour* [Morton or the Grand Tour], 1835; 1975.

(Vols. 11-15 contain five volumes usually referred to as *Lebensbilder aus der westlichen Hemisphäre*; the title of the English translation is *Life in the New World*.)

Vol. 11: *George Howard's Esq. Brautfahrt* [Courtship of George Howard Esq.], 1834; 1976.

Vol. 12: *Ralph Doughby's Esq. Brautfahrt* [Courtship of Ralph Doughby Esq.], 1835; 1976.

Vol. 13/14: *Pflanzerleben* Parts I and II, *Die Farbigen* [Life of a Planter, Colored Women], 1836; 1976.

Vol. 15: *Nathan, der Squatter-Regulator, oder der erste Amerikaner in Texas* [Nathan, the Squatter-Regulator or, The First American in Texas], 1837; 1977.

Vol. 16/17: *Das Kajütenbuch oder Nationale Charakeristiken* [The Cabin Book or, National Characteristics], 1841; 1977.

*Vol. 18/19/20: *Süden und Norden* [South and North], 1842/43; 1978.

Vol. 21/22/23: *Die deutsch-amerikanischen Wahlverwandtschaften* [German-American Elective Affinities], 1839/40; 1982.

Das Kajütenbuch oder Nationale Charakteristiken, edited by Alexander Ritter, Stuttgart: Reclam, 1982. This fine edition includes very helpful annotations, a detailed introduction to the author and his work, a new interpretation, and a bibliography of secondary materials pertaining to Sealsfield's works in general and the *Kajütenbuch*.

The United States of North America as They Are contains an introduction in English by William E. Wright. New York, London: Johnson Repr., 1970.

A new edition of Sealsfield's works, edited by Alexander Ritter and Günter Schnitzler, will be published by Insel starting in 1986.

English editions originally published in German

Some of the editions listed below have been republished as late as 1886. Only the first of these editions are mentioned here.

*Life in the New World, or Sketches of American Society. Transl. by G. Hebbe and J. Mackay. New York: Winchester, 1844. (English translation of the *Lebensbilder* cycle.)

The Cabin Book; or Sketches of Life in Texas. Transl. by C. F. Mersch. New York: Winchester, 1844. (English translation of *Das Kajütenbuch.*)

The Cabin Book. Transl. by Sarah Powell. London, 1852.

Rambleton; A Romance of Fashionable Life in New York, during the Great Speculation of 1836. Transl. by S., New York: Winchester, 1844. (English Translation of *Die Deutsch-Amerikanischen Wahlverwandtschaften.*) Republished in 1846 under the title of *Flirtations in America.*

North and South; or, Scenes and Adventures in Mexico. Transl. by J.T.H. New York: Winchester, 1844.

Selections of Sealsfield's works appeared in *Blackwood's Edinburgh Magazine* from 1843 to 1845 in translations by Frederick Hardman. These selections include parts of Sealsfield's *Virey* in vol. 57 (1845), in three installments under the title *Mexico in 1812.*

Only one, highly unsatisfactory edition of Sealsfield's fiction has recently been published in English: Ulrich S. Carrington, ed., *The Making of an American. An Adaptation of Memorable Tales by Charles Sealsfield.* Dallas: SMU Press, 1974.

B. SMALLER WORKS

Sealsfield scholars have attributed a number of smaller works, including articles, to Sealsfield. In many cases, however, Sealsfield's authorship of these pieces remains highly doubtful. The following listing includes only those works for which Sealsfield's penmanship is least questionable.

"Christopher Bärenhaüter." *Transatlantische Reisseskizzen und Christophorus Bärenhäuter.* Zürich: Orell, Fußli, 1834, 75-166.

Die Grabesschuld. Posthumously edited by Alfred Meissner, Leipzig, 1873.

"A Night on the Banks of Tennessee." *New-York Mirror, and Ladies' Literary Gazette* 31 October 1829 and 7 November 1929.

"Early Impressions: A Fragment." *Atlantic Souvenir* 1830: 149-167. Repr. in *The Journal of English and Germanic Philology* 55 (1956): 100-16, edited by Karl J. R. Arndt.

"Scenes in Poland." *Englishman's Magazine* London, 1831: 26-32 and 170-90.

"My Little Grey Landlord." *Englishman's Magazine* 1831: 268-80.

"Three Meetings on the King's Highway." *Englishman's Magazine* 1831: 401-10.

"Borelli and Menotti." *Englishman's Magazine* 1831: 608-15.

CRITICAL WORKS CITED
AND WORKS ABOUT SEALSFIELD

Arndt, Karl J. R. "Sealsfield's Early Reception in England and America." *American German Review* 18 (1943): 176-95.

Arndt, Karl J. R. "Charles Sealsfield. 'The Greatest American Author'." *Proceedings of the American Antiquarian Society for October 1964.* Worchester, MA (1965): 248-59.

_____ . "Plagiarism: Sealsfield or Simms?" *Modern Language Notes* 69 (1954): 577-81.

Ashby, Nanette M. *Charles Sealsfield: "The Greatest American Author." A Study of Literary Piracy and Promotion in the 19th Century.* Diss. Stanford Univ., 1939. A special edition of this thesis was published in 1980 by the Charles Sealsfield Society, Stuttgart, Fed. Rep. of Germany.

Billington, Ray Allen. "Foreword" to *The Making of an American. An Adaptation of Memorable Tales by Charles Sealsfield.* Ed. Ulrich S. Carrington. Dallas: SMU Press, 1974. ix-xii.

_____ . *The Protestant Crusade, 1800-1860: A Study of the Origins of American Nativism.* New York: Macmillan, 1938.

Castle, Eduard. *Das Geheimnis des großen Unbekannten. Charles Sealsfield—Carl Postl. Die Quellenschriften.* Vienna: Wiener Bibliophilen-Gesellschaft, 1943. A rare book containing many of the materials on which Castle's biography of Sealsfield, published in 1952, is based.

_____ . *Der große Unbekannte. Das Leben von Charles Sealsfield (Karl Postl).* Vienna, Munich: Manutius, 1952. Although very deficient in many respects and somewhat influenced by National-Socialist ideology, this book is still the only serious biographical treatment of Sealsfield.

_____ . *Der große Unbekannte. Das Leben von Charles Sealsfield (Karl Postl)*. *Briefe und Aktenstücke*. Wien: Werner, 1955. Contains many of the letters and other personal documents on which Castle's biography is based.

Cowie, Alexander. *The Rise of the American Novel*. New York: American Book, 1948.

Dallmann, William Paul. *The Spirit of America as Interpreted in the Works of Charles Sealsfield*. St. Louis, MO: n.p., 1935.

Doerry, Karl W. "Three Versions of America: Sealsfield, Gerstäcker, and May." *Yearbook of German-American Studies* 16 (1981): 39-49.

Filson, John. *The Discovery, Settlement and present State of Kentucke . . . .* Wilmington: Adams, 1784; rpt. Ann Arbor: UMI, 1966.

Friesen, Gerhard. *The German Panoramic Novel of the 19th Century*. Bern, Frankfurt/Main: Lang, 1972.

Ganilh, Anthony. *Mexico versus Texas, A Descriptive Novel, Most of the Characters of Which Consist of Living Persons. By a Texan*. Philadelphia: Siegfried, 1838.

Gaston, Edwin W., Jr. *The Early Novel of the Southwest*. Albuquerque, NM: Univ. of N.M. Press, 1961.

Grünzweig, Walter. "The Italian Sky in the Republic of Letters: Charles Sealsfield and Timothy Flint as Early Writers of the American West." *Yearbook of German-American Studies* 17 (1982): 1-20.

_____ . " 'Where Millions of Happy People Might Live Peacefully': Jackson's Westen in Charles Sealsfield's *Tokeah; or the White Rose*." *Amerikastudien/American Studies* 28 (1983) 219-36.

Heller, Otto, and Theodore H. Leon *The Language of Charles Sealsfield. A Study in Atypical Usage*. Washington University Studies—New Series, No. 11. St. Louis, MO, 1941.

Heller, Otto. "Some Sources of Sealsfield." *Modern Philology* 7 (1909/10): 587-92.

Hill, Murray G. "Some of Longfellow's Sources for the Second Part of *Evangeline*." *PMLA* 31 (1916): 160-80.

Jefferson, Thomas. *Notes on the State of Virginia*. Ed. Thomas Perkins Abernethy. Gloucester, MA: Smith, 1976.

Pearce, Roy Harvey. *Savagism and Civilization: A Study of the Indian and the American Mind*. Rev. ed. Baltimore: The Johns Hopkins Press, 1965.

Riese, Teut Andreas. "Man's Rebirth in the Wilderness. The Immigrant Writer's View." *Vistas of a Continent. Concepts of Nature in America*. Ed. T. A. Riese. Heidelberg: Winter, 1979.

Ritter, Alexander. *Darstellung und Funktion der Landschaft in den Amerika-Romanen von Charles Sealsfield (Karl Postl). Eine Studie zum Prosa-Roman der deutschen und amerikanischen Literatur in der ersten Hälfte des 19. Jahrhunderts.* Diss. U of Kiel. 1969. Printed by the Charles Sealsfield Society, Stuttgart, 1970.

—————— . "Charles Sealsfield's gesellschaftspolitische Vorstellungen und ihre dichterische Gestaltung als Romanzyklus." *Jahrbuch der Deutschen Schillergesellschaft* 17 (1973): 395-414.

—————— . "Charles Sealsfield. Literaturgeschichtliche Standortbestimmung und philologischer Auftrag." *Deutsche Dichter des 19. Jahrhunderts*, Ed. B.v. Wiese. Second Edition. Berlin: Schmidt, 1979. 98-127.

—————— . "Charles Sealsfield: Politischer Emigrant, freier Schriftstellar und die Doppelkrise von Amerika-Utopie und Gesellschaft im 19. Jahrhundert." *Freiburger Universitätsblätter* 75 (1982): 43-64.

—————— . "Charles Sealsfield's Madonnas Of(f) the Trails' im Roman *Das Kajütenbuch*. Oder: Zur epischen Zähmung der Frauen als Stereotype in der amerikanischen Südstaatenepik zwischen 1820 und 1850." *Yearbook of German-American Studies* 18 (1983): 91-112.

Sammons, Jeffrey L. "Land of Limited Possibilities: America in the Nineteenth-Century German Novel." *Yale Review* 67 (1978): 35-52.

Schmidt-Dengler, Wendelin: "Charles Sealsfield. *Das Kajütenbuch* (1841)." *Romane und Erzählungen zwischen Romantik und Realismus.* Ed. Paul Michael Lützeler. Stuttgart: Reclam, 1983. 314-34.

Schüppen, Franz. *Charles Sealsfield. Karl Postl. Ein österreichischer Erzähler der Biedermeierzeit im Spannungsfeld von Alter und Neuer Welt.* Frankfurt/M./Bern: Lang, 1981.

Sengle, Friedrich. "Karl Postl. Pseud. Charles Sealsfield. (1793-1864)." *Biedermeierzeit. Deutsche Literatur in Spannungsfeld zwischen Restauration und Revolution. 1815-1848.* Vol. 3: *Die Dichter.* Stuttgart, 1980. 752-814.

Steinecke, Hartmut. "'Literatur als Aufklärungsmittel'. Zur Neubestimmung der Werke Charles Sealsfield zwischen Österreich, Deutschland und Amerika." *Die österreichische Literatur. Ihr Profil im 19. Jahrhundert. (1830-1880).* Graz, 1982. 399-422.

Uhlendorf, Bernhard A. *Charles Sealsfield. Ethnic Elements and National Problems in His Works.* Chicago: n.p., 1922.

Ward, John William. *Andrew Jackson: Symbol for an Age.* New York: Oxford Univ. Press, 1955.

Weiss, Walter: "Der Zusammenhang zwischen Amerika-Thematik und Erzählkunst bei Charles Sealsfield (Karl Postl)." *Lit. wiss. Jahrbuch der Görres-Gesellschaft* 8 (1967): 95-118.

74280012 $\frac{42}{64}$ p640

PT 2516 .S4 Z863 1985
Grunzweig.   71748
Charles Sealsfield
WITHDRAWN

Date Due